BORIS YELTSIN

Boris Yeltsin
AND THE
REBIRTH OF
RUSSIA

STEVEN OTFINOSKI

THE MILLBROOK PRESS
BROOKFIELD, CONNECTICUT

All photographs courtesy of Bettmann except p. 95,
courtesy of Wide World

Library of Congress Cataloging-in-Publication Data
Otfinoski, Steven.
Boris Yeltsin and the rebirth of Russia / Steven Otfinoski.
p.   cm.
Includes bibliographical references and index.
Summary: A biography of the president of Russsia, a maverick
politician and key figure in the formation of the Commonwealth
of Independent States.
ISBN 1-56294-478-9
1. Yeltsin, Boris Nikolayevich, 1931-   —Juvenile literature.
2. Presidents—Russia (Federation)—Biography—Juvenile literature.
3. Politicians—Soviet Union—Biography—Juvenile literature.
4. Soviet Union—Politics and government—1985-1991—Juvenile
literature.   5. Russia (Federation)—Politics and government—1991-
—Juvenile literature. [1. Yeltsin, Boris Nikolayevich, 1931-
2. Presidents—Russia (Federation)]   I. Title.
DK290.3.Y45084   1995
947.086—dc20   94-20296   CIP   AC

Published by The Millbrook Press, Inc.
2 Old New Milford Road, Brookfield, Connecticut 06804

CONTENTS

BORIS YELTSIN

CHAPTER ONE

"RUSSIA WILL BE FREE"

Most coups d'état are announced with gunfire and tanks. This one arrived quietly in a black limousine. The limousine drove through the quiet, pre-dawn streets of Moscow on Monday, August 19, 1991, and pulled up outside the official Tass News agency. Leonid Kravchenko, who once ran Tass and now was a member of Mikhail Gorbachev's government, climbed out with a briefcase full of announcements. A short time later, the Soviet Union and the world were told via television, radio, and news wire that Gorbachev was "unable for health reasons" to perform his duties as leader of the country. The reins of government were being passed to the State Committee for the State of Emergency in the USSR.

This eight-man "committee" had hoped that Gorbachev himself would have announced his resignation. But when they approached him about it twelve hours earlier at his vacation home on the Black Sea he told them to "go to hell."[1] So the conspirators put him and his family under house arrest and proceeded with their plans.

In fact, there was nothing wrong with Gorbachev's health. There was something wrong with his judgment, however. Only the previous year he had appointed to high positions in his government five of the eight men who were now betraying him. They included his vice president, prime minister, and defense minister. These men were opposed to the reforms that Gorbachev was imposing on the Communist system they had grown up and thrived under. They wanted to turn back the clock and return the Soviet Union to hard-line communism.

As the morning wore on, troops and tanks began to fill the downtown streets of Moscow. People came out of their homes and offices to stare in disbelief, and then anger. They put up no resistance. Gorbachev was their leader, but the promised economic reforms for improving their lives had been painfully slow in coming. Would they now put their lives on the line for a cause they were rapidly losing faith in?

The coup leaders were counting on the people's lack of commitment. They were also counting on the self-interest of most of the country's politicians, who would hesitate to condemn the conspirators' actions as long as there was any chance of their succeeding. The one person they didn't count on was Boris Yeltsin.

Yeltsin was the newly elected president of Russia. After Gorbachev, he was the most important politician in the Soviet Union and a firm supporter of democratic reform. Yeltsin awoke to the news of the takeover at his home outside Moscow. Despite the danger, he decided to go into work. He kissed his wife and daughters goodbye and drove into Moscow. Shortly after, special police arrived at his house to arrest him. They were forty minutes too late.

Yeltsin's office was in a large, white marble government building—the so-called White House—that housed the Russian parliament, the first popularly-elected governing body in Russia's thousand-year history. The coup leaders needed to shut down the White House to make their seizure of power complete. They preferred to do it peacefully, but they were prepared to use force.

At the White House, Yeltsin was joined by other political leaders who opposed the coup. Former Interior Minister Vadim Bakhatin and others urged Yeltsin to declare himself in command of all army units in the Russian republic. Yeltsin, fearing a civil war, hesitated. His colleagues quickly convinced him that he had to take action or the coup would succeed.

Shortly after noon, Yeltsin, now resolute, decided it was time to make his own statement to the people of the Soviet Union. While a small crowd watched, he climbed onto one of the tanks parked in front of the White House and boldly addressed them. Yeltsin told his listeners that "the clouds of terror and dictatorship are gathering over the whole country. They must not be allowed to bring eternal night."[2] He branded the coup illegal and called for a general strike to end it. When he was done, he climbed down from the tank and went back into the parliament building.

Word of Yeltsin's courageous speech started to spread. People across the Soviet Union began to demonstrate against the conspirators. World leaders called Yeltsin in his office to get further news of what was happening in Moscow and to offer him their support. Over the next two days, Yeltsin spent hours on the phone with U.S. President George Bush, British Prime Minister John Major, and other Western heads of state.

Meanwhile, the coup leaders were worried. The longer Yeltsin and the other resistance leaders stayed at large, the harder it would be to enforce their author-

ity. They had already showed signs of indecisiveness. At a press conference later in the day they appeared nervous and unsure of themselves. They changed their story about Gorbachev's resignation, saying he might return to power after regaining his health. Their fumbling was beginning to make them look like clowns in the eyes of the world. They had to either show some strength or give up the game.

An assault on the White House was planned for 3 A.M. Tuesday, the second day of the coup. However, the parliament building was now surrounded by several thousand people who had responded to Yeltsin's call to arms. They acted as a human shield to protect the building and the people inside. The generals in charge of the military operation knew they would have a bloodbath . They refused to carry out the assault.

As day two dawned, the coup leaders were no longer in control of the only means of communications. The White House had become the heart and lifeblood of the resistance. Television cameras had been set up to transmit President Yeltsin's impassioned speech to both the uncommitted public and those defending the coup.

"I appeal to you, soldiers and officers of Russia," Yeltsin said. "Do not let yourselves be turned into blind weapons to defend privileges. In this difficult hour,

■■■■■■ President Yeltsin considers his next move from inside the barricaded Russian parliament building during the 1991 coup. The armed bodyguard indicates the danger Yeltsin is in after his defiant stand against the conspirators.

distinguish real truth from lies. Do not dishonor Russia by shedding the blood of your own people. The days of the plotters are numbered. Law and constitutional order will be victorious. Russia will be free."[3]

Yeltsin's courage in the face of tyranny was contagious. By Tuesday night, thousands of Muscovites had built barricades on the roads leading to the White House. When tanks tried to clear the barricades, they were met with resistance. In one clash, two young men were killed. The coup had drawn its first blood.

By the morning of the third day the State Committee for the State of Emergency was deep in its own state of emergency. Their military support, never very solid, was dribbling away. Hundreds of politicians who had been afraid to make a stand against them were now joining the masses in opposing them.

The Russian parliament opened at 10 o'clock that morning. Boris Yeltsin made a speech, condemning the coup leaders. By midafternoon, he announced that some of the conspirators were on their way to the airport to flee the country. Several government leaders were dispatched to track them down and to bring Gorbachev back from his vacation home where he had been held prisoner.

By evening all the coup leaders but one were back in Moscow and under arrest. Interior Minister Boris Pugo had shot himself. It was the last act of violence in an ill-fated coup that had lasted less than 72 hours. But if it had not been for the courage and leadership of one man, the takeover might have succeeded.

The Communist bureaucrats hungry for power were ill-suited for the role of revolutionaries. But Boris Yeltsin was tailor-made for the role of the hero of his country. It was something he had been preparing for all his life.

CHAPTER TWO

A BIT OF
A HOOLIGAN

Struggling against overwhelming odds was something that came naturally to Boris Yeltsin. The struggles began from the day he was born, or to be more precise, on the day of his baptism.

Boris Nikolayevich Yeltsin was born in the Russian village of Butko on February 1, 1931. Butko lay 155 miles (250 kilometers) south of Sverdlovsk, the capital city of Sverdlovsk, a Soviet province nestled in the Ural Mountains, which divide the European plain of Russia from the West Siberian Plain. Despite the fact that the Communist government had forbidden religion, people in remote areas, such as the Urals, clung stubbornly to their Russian Orthodox Christian beliefs.

Shortly after his birth, Boris was taken to church to be baptized. It was a Russian custom for the parents of the baptized child to offer the priest a glass of home-brewed alcohol as a gift. This is what nearly cost him his life, as Yeltsin recalled in his autobiography:

> Since my turn did not come until the afternoon, the priest, having drunk many toasts, could barely stand. . . . [he] dropped me into the tub

and, being drawn into an argument with a member of the congregation, forgot to take me out. At first, my parents, who were standing at some distance from the baptismal font, didn't know what had happened. When they finally realized what was going on, my mother screamed, leapt forward, and fished me out. . . .

They then shook the water out of me. The priest was not particularly worried. He said, "Well if he can survive such an ordeal, it means he's a good, tough lad—and I name him Boris." * [1]

To survive in rural Russia during Joseph Stalin's first years in power, a child had to be tough. Stalin ordered all privately owned farms to be taken over by the Communist state in a process called "collectivization." Those farmers who resisted were driven into exile, killed, or starved to death.

The Yeltsins, who were barely eking out a living on their own, were forced to move to a collective farm called a *kolkhoz.* The family struggled to make the farm a success. Then their only horse died, and they couldn't plow their fields. When their cow died, Boris's grandfather hired himself out to neighbors as a carpenter, cabinetmaker, and builder of brick stoves.

Boris's father, Nikolai Ignatyevich, also decided to quit farming and went to work building a potash plant in the neighboring province of Perm. The work was steady, but the family continued to live in grinding poverty. They moved into a long wooden barracks with

* Boris means "battler" or "warrior" in Old Russian.

twenty other families. This crude housing was supposed to be only temporary, but the Yeltsins lived there in near squalor for ten years. There was no indoor plumbing, and water was drawn from a well. Boris, his two siblings, parents, and grandfather all lived in one room. They slept on the floor at night huddled around a goat for warmth. The goat also provided milk for the children.

Perhaps the worst aspect of life in the barracks was the nearly total absence of privacy. Yet young Boris adapted surprisingly well to the communal conditions. They instilled in him a love for group living and a need to be surrounded by people. Even as an adult, Yeltsin could not stand to be alone for any length of time.

Another character trait he developed at an early age was a strong sense of responsibility. From the age of six, Boris virtually ran the household while his father worked at the factory and his mother, Klavdiya Vasilyeana, worked as a seamstress. He watched over his baby sister and brother, tended the vegetable garden, cooked meals, and cleaned up afterward. His mother taught him to sew, an unusual skill for a Russian boy. In summer he would mow grass with her on farms outside of the village for extra money. He remained close to his mother all his life.

His relationship with his father was not as warm, although he never ceased to love him. Nikolai Yeltsin was quick-tempered, rough, independent, and had a keen sense of integrity—all traits that his son would inherit. A self-taught inventor, Nikolai designed an automatic bricklayer but was never able to complete a working model. During World War II, he was commissioned to build a new factory, but when he found the design he was given was defective, he refused to build it.

▬▬▬▬▬▬▬▬▬ This Russian village is
typical of thousands of villages across Russia
in the years following the Russian Revolution.
The photograph was taken in 1921, ten years
before Yeltsin's birth in the village of Butko.

Nikolai was as uncompromising with his son as he was with others. "My father's chief instrument for teaching good behavior was the strap," recalled Yeltsin, "and he walloped me good and proper for any lapses. . . . I always clenched my teeth and did not make a sound, which infuriated him."[2]

When he reached the age of fifteen, Boris decided he had taken all the punishment he was going to. One day, he grabbed the belt from his father's hand and cried, "That's it! From now on I'm educating myself!"[3]

Boris's brand of self-education was often risky and dangerous. He was by his own admission a "little bit of a hooligan."[4] At age eleven, as World War II was raging around them, Boris and some friends decided to steal a couple of grenades in order to study them and make their own. Ammunition was warehoused in a local church, and Boris volunteered to break in and steal the grenades.

"That night I crept through three layers of barbed wire, and while the sentry was on the other side of the building, I filed through the mesh on a window and climbed inside," Yeltsin recalled.[5] Risking certain death if the sentry spotted him, Boris crawled back to his friends with two hand grenades.

"We went to a forest about forty miles away," he continued. "I told the other boys to take cover a hundred yards off; then I put the grenade on a stone, knelt down, and hit it with a hammer. I didn't realize I had to remove the fuse."[6]

The grenade exploded, mangling the thumb and forefinger of his left hand. By the time his friends got him to a hospital, gangrene had already set in. The surgeons amputated the two fingers.

This handicap didn't stop the energetic youth from pursuing sports in school, especially volleyball, which became his passion. On the athletic field and in the classroom Boris became a leader and, in some cases, a ringleader. In the fifth grade he decided to turn the tables on a teacher he didn't like by convincing the entire class to jump out the first-floor window while the teacher was out of the room. She returned to an empty classroom.

Boris asked if he could speak at his primary school graduation. Before the stunned assembly of faculty, parents, and students, he condemned his homeroom teacher for "cruel, unusual punishment" and demanded that she be dismissed.[7] Instead, Boris was expelled and told he could not continue on to secondary school. Not ready to accept this ruling without a fight, he went to the city educational department to plead his case. Boris was allowed to continue his education, and the teacher in question was eventually fired. It was the first of many political battles to come from which he would emerge the victor.

Boris went on to Sverdlovsk's Pushkin School, where he spent as much time on the volleyball court as he did in class. If Boris had a nickname in high school, it might have been "The Organizer." He was always organizing games, after-school activities, and even summer vacations. The summer after ninth grade, he got a group of friends to trek into the wilderness to find the course of the river Yaiva. They got lost in the Urals forest and survived for days on berries and mushrooms. The group returned downriver on a boat they traded for their remaining supplies and promptly got lost again. Boris contracted typhoid fever from drinking swamp water and later spent three months in the hospital. Such behavior would set a pattern for the future. He would continue throughout his life to push himself to the maximum in the face of a challenge, risking his health and sometimes his very life in the process.

In 1949, Boris graduated from high school with top honors and applied to enter the Urals Polytechnic Institute. He decided to follow in his father's footsteps and study civil engineering. The Institute accepted him as a student, but Boris's grandfather told him he had to prove himself before he could enter the school. He challenged his grandson to build a bathhouse with his own hands. Boris dutifully undertook the task, even cutting down the pine trees for the foundation. When Boris was finished, his grandfather was pleased with the results and said he was ready to go to school.

The Urals Polytechnic Institute was one of the largest schools in the Soviet Union, with 30,000 students. Boris entered the Construction Department and plunged into a punishing schedule. He attended classes early in the day, played volleyball for six to eight hours, and studied at night. Politics seemed the furthest thing from his mind, and he shunned ideological arguments. The only protests he organized had to do with the personal rights of students and never involved the world outside the university gates. In the last days of the dictatorial reign of Stalin this was probably a wise course for any young man or woman with professional ambitions.

Most of Boris's ambitions seemed confined to the volleyball court. He was not only a varsity player at school, but he played in Sverdlovsk's senior league, roughly the equivalent of a major-league sports team in the United States. As a team member, he traveled all over the Soviet Union playing volleyball with other teams. He even slept with a volleyball on his pillow.

Volleyball nearly proved his undoing. "I fell ill with tonsillitis," he wrote in his autobiography. "I had a temperature of 104 degrees, but I still went on training. My heart couldn't stand it. My pulse was 150 when I collapsed and was taken to hospital."[8] True to form, he escaped from the hospital, went home to recover, and returned to school to play volleyball. "I had taken a colossal risk, but it paid off," he wrote.[9] These words would be repeated again and again over the course of a public career that at times seemed as reckless as it was remarkable.

An extrovert in any group, Boris could be painfully shy in more intimate encounters. Despite his wide circle of friends, he had no close companion with whom he shared his inner life. When it came to romance, he was something of a fool. To prove his love for one girl, he leaped into a chilly lake with his clothes on. He found out later that the girl was in love with someone else.

Then he met Naina (Naya) Girin, an attractive fellow student who was everything he was not—"modest, charming and gentle."[10] They dated for nearly four years. At graduation in 1955, Boris got a job as a construction boss in Sverdlovsk, while Naya was assigned a job at Orenburg, nearly 450 miles (725 kilometers) to the southwest. They decided they would part and see if their feelings for each other were the same after a year's time. While Naya pined in Orenburg, Boris plunged into his new career in construction with the same gusto he had displayed on the athletic field.

CHAPTER THREE

THE MAN WHO GOT THINGS DONE

If Yeltsin's grandfather made him build a brick bath-house before he could enter the Urals Polytechnic, nobody forced him to do what he did on his first job after finishing school—nobody but Yeltsin himself.

Instead of starting work as a construction foreman at the Urals Heavy Pipe Construction Trust, he insisted on spending his first year on the job learning each of the twelve trades of the men who would be working under him. To complete this Herculean task, Yeltsin would have to master one skill a month. It took the average worker at least six months to master his skill. Yeltsin, once again, pushed himself to the limits of human endurance to become in one brief year, among other things, a stone mason, carpenter, painter, cement layer, and crane operator.

"Even though the workers laughed at a young graduate's enthusiasm for getting his hands dirty," Yeltsin later recalled, "they helped me, encouraged me, and gave me moral support."[1]

When the year was up, Yeltsin reported to his superiors and announced he was ready to start work as a foreman. His superiors, perhaps as a mean joke on this all-too-earnest young man, asked him to build a small firing hut where building materials such as bricks were baked and hardened. This would prove he was ready for the job. Yeltsin refused. He had passed his own demanding test and didn't need to prove himself to anyone else. His obstinacy got him assigned to the lowest foreman job.

Yeltsin didn't complain; he went to work. He did complain, however, when he heard that company workers were being mistreated. He met with them and then brought their complaints to management. Again, his independence was not appreciated. He was punished and given the roughest construction sites to work on. He didn't seem to mind. This burly, tough man from the Urals was a confirmed workaholic decades before the term was coined. He was totally dedicated to the task at hand and would spend days at the work site.

His first year on the job also proved meaningful for his relationship with Naya. They realized their love was stronger than the distance that separated them. The couple were married in 1956 in Sverdlovsk with all their college friends present. After a brief honeymoon, Naya went to work at the Institute of Waterways in Sverdlovsk. She remained there for twenty-nine years, working her way up to the position of chief engineer.

Yeltsin loved his wife but, by his own admission, spent little time at home. In his autobiography he devotes all of one sentence to his marriage during this period: "By this time I was married, and my wife and I lived right next to the construction site."[2] Their first daughter, Lena, was born in 1957, and their second daughter, Tanya, arrived two years later. Yeltsin confesses he was so busy with his work that he has few memories of their childhood years. Naya let him work on Saturdays, but would not allow it on Sundays. This became, and remained, the one day of the week that Yeltsin spent quality time with his family.

As sympathetic as he was to the needs of his workers, Yeltsin was a hard taskmaster. He drove his men as hard as he drove himself. Perhaps because he had taken the time and energy to learn their jobs, the workers respected him, despite his toughness. They also respected his integrity. While other foremen put their relatives and friends in soft, well-paid positions, Yeltsin would not even help his brother-in-law get a minor promotion, declaring the man was "not ready yet."[3] At the same time, Yeltsin could quietly give part of his salary to a woman worker he hardly knew who was unjustly fired, and then help her get her job back.

Yeltsin's devotion to work didn't appear to help him financially. Naya had to keep working as an engineer while raising their daughters just to make ends meet. But the lack of material success mattered little to Boris Yeltsin. In a way, he was a model of what a good Communist was supposed to be—totally dedicated to his work, selfless, and considerate of those less fortunate.

Yet few Communists met this criteria. In the bureaucracy that Stalin created, the few at the top had all the privileges and only paid lip service to the Communist creed of brotherhood and equality. Stalin's successor, Nikita Khrushchev, who came to power in 1956, tried to improve the lot of the average Soviet citizen, while leaving much of the corrupt Stalinist system in place. One of Khrushchev's main areas of reform was housing. This gave work to a new generation of builders and engineers like Yeltsin, who, perhaps remembering his

own shabby house in his childhood, put all his energies into building better homes.

At this time, Yeltsin took an uncharacteristic step to help his career. He joined the Communist party. The party represented the elite of the Soviet Union. Party membership was a key that unlocked the door to power and influence. Yeltsin had resisted this easy route to success as long as he could. Although he was never a wholehearted believer in Soviet-style communism, he realized that he had gone as far as he could on his own. To get any farther, he would have to join the party. There was simply no other way.

As part of his application to the party, Yeltsin was interviewed by the chief accountant of the construction directorate he worked under. The man did not like Yeltsin and tried to trip him up with some tough questions. The plan backfired, as Yeltsin later remembered:

> He asked me on what page of which volume of *Das Kapital* Marx refers to commodity-money relationships. Assuming that he had never read Marx closely and had, of course, no idea of either the volume or the page number in question, and that he didn't even know what commodity-money relationships were, I imme-

■■■■■■ **Nikita Khrushchev, here at the height of his power in 1959, tried to reform the Soviet state he inherited from Joseph Stalin. His efforts to improve housing conditions created plenty of work for young engineers like Boris Yeltsin.**

diately answered, half-jokingly, "Volume Two, page 387." What's more I said it quickly, without pausing for thought. To which he replied with a sage expression, "Well done. You know your Marx well."[4]

The hypocrisy of Communist officials who didn't know the tenets of their own political system bothered Yeltsin. So did the fact that these bureaucrats lived lives of privilege while the great masses of the Soviet people could barely get by.

Whatever reservations Yeltsin's superiors had about him, they could not deny that he was a "man who got things done."[5] From foreman of construction crews for factory workshops, apartment blocks, and schools, Yeltsin rose, by age thirty-two, to be the manager of a huge state construction company that manufactured and built prefabricated housing for the city of Sverdlovsk. Some twenty thousand people worked under him. As a manager, Yeltsin could see how the red tape and constant interference of the party was hindering his industry and the entire economy.

━━━ As he built his career in construction, Boris Yeltsin had little time for his family. By his own admission, he has few memories of the childhoods of his two daughters. This 1989 photograph shows him with his wife Naina at the breakfast table —probably the most time they spend together even these days.

It was perhaps a desire to reform a system that desperately needed it that led Yeltsin to get involved in politics. When an invitation came in 1969 to head the construction section of the Sverdlovsk provincial party committee, Yeltsin accepted the job. He was now a full-time Communist party official. Little has been written about the seven years that Yeltsin labored as a section chief and later a secretary of the Sverdlovsk provincial committee. It is safe to say that the same hard work, leadership, and integrity that made him stand out from his associates in the construction business eventually brought him to the attention of the party leadership in Moscow.

That leadership had changed drastically in 1964 when Nikita Khrushchev was ousted from power by his lieutenants and replaced by his right-hand man, Leonid Brezhnev. Under Brezhnev, most of Khrushchev's reforms came to an end. Corruption and moral decay became the Soviet standard, as Brezhnev promoted family and friends to important positions in government.

In 1976, Yeltsin was sent to Moscow to attend a two-week course at the Academy of Social Sciences. To his surprise, he was summoned to appear before members of the Central Committee, one of the highest governing bodies in the Soviet Union. Yeltsin was questioned for some time, for what reason he could not fathom. Then he was taken by two committee members into the Kremlin and brought face-to-face with Brezhnev himself. To Yeltsin's astonishment, Brezhnev offered him the position of first secretary of the provincial committee. First secretary of a province was roughly the American equivalent of governor of a state. Brezhnev explained that the present secretary was being promoted to the Central Committee. Although the job of first provincial secretary was usually offered to the second secretary, this man was found unsuitable for the responsibility. After hearing Brezhnev out, Yeltsin accepted the job. His rapid rise to this position of power was almost unprecedented. Usually a party official waited twenty to thirty years for such a promotion. Yeltsin had been a party member for only fifteen years.

On November 2, 1976, the full assembly, or plenum, of the Sverdlovsk provincial committee met and unanimously accepted Yeltsin as their new leader. Yeltsin gave a brief acceptance speech. The central message he conveyed was one he had adhered to in his fourteen years in the construction industry. "We should above all, be concerned about *people* and their welfare," he said, "since if you treat people well they will respond with improved performance in whatever their occupation may be."[6] As first secretary of Sverdlovsk, Boris Yeltsin would give new life and meaning to these words.

CHAPTER FOUR

THE MAVERICK OF SVERDLOVSK

Sverdlovsk was an extremely important province in the Russian republic of the Soviet Union. It had the third-highest output of industrial products in the country and was a major center of the defense industry. At the time Yeltsin assumed leadership, Sverdlovsk was the third largest of the Russian provinces, with a population of 1.2 million spread over 80,000 square miles (207,000 square kilometers).

The challenge of running this immense region was a daunting one, but Yeltsin met it with characteristic enthusiasm. He ran Sverdlovsk as he had run his construction sites, with boundless energy, total commitment, and the fervor of a reformer. He made a vow to visit the province's sixty-three towns and forty-five large villages once every two years—a promise he kept. These trips were hardly publicity junkets. Yeltsin would visit schools and factories, making speeches and meeting with local officials and ordinary citizens. He listened carefully to their problems and concerns. Out of these fact-finding trips, Yeltsin shaped a bold agenda for change.

One issue that lay close to his heart was housing. He was disturbed to see many of the people in his province living in the same squalid, decrepit wooden huts he and his family had endured for years. He decided to provide new, modern housing for these people. To do this, he had to freeze the long waiting list on housing for a year. Many of Sverdlovsk's citizens had been waiting for new apartments for some time and were angry with Yeltsin for serving the needs of the poorer people before them. As would happen at nearly every step of his political career, this move made Yeltsin as many enemies as it did friends.

Another area in which Sverdlovsk was woefully lacking was roads. The city of Sverdlovsk was in the center of the province, while the industrial towns lay to the north. To transport goods and people between the North and the capital took ten days by railroad, because there was no direct roadway. The 220-mile (350-kilometer) distance was fraught with all kinds of natural obstacles—mountains, rivers, and swamps. When Yeltsin proposed that a highway be built north from Sverdlovsk, the central government turned him down. Such a project, they said, would be far too costly. So Yeltsin decided to take matters into his own hands. He financed the highway locally, relying on each municipality to pay for and build the section of the road that would pass through it. The project took nearly ten years and was the crowning achievement of Yeltsin's administration.

On the day when the Sverdlovsk-Serov Highway, as it was called, was supposed to be completed, Yeltsin loaded all the local party bosses onto a bus and made the maiden journey up the new highway. Some bosses had not finished their section of the roadway on time.

Yeltsin, ever the tough taskmaster, told each negligent boss to get off the bus at his unfinished stretch of road. He left them there to get back to the nearest town on their own.

It was a humiliating lesson that Yeltsin later claimed to have regretted. "To make senior city officials get out of the bus for all to see is not very kind," he wrote. But from a practical point of view "it worked."[1] The party bosses were never late for a deadline again.

Yeltsin's dictatorial style was successful, but it was not popular among the old-time party bureaucrats, called in Russian *apparatchiki.* These officials of the Communist party were used to special privileges. While the common people spent hours waiting in line to buy basic foods and goods, apparatchiki shopped at special stores where all sorts of delicacies were available at reasonable prices. Yeltsin saw this as a gross injustice. He closed down these special stores and clamped down on other party privileges. The apparatchiki were furious. One old Sverdlovsk party member expressed the opinion of many of his colleagues when he said, "As a Party man, he [Yeltsin] was a zero."[2]

How did this fiery reformer who broke all the rules of doing business manage to keep his job in the Brezhnev era of corruption? English journalist and Yeltsin biographer John Morrison gives two explanations. One, for all its authoritarianism, the Communist government in the Soviet Union had grown fat and lazy. Brezhnev, growing older and more doddering each year, left the provincial secretaries pretty much alone. Most followed the well-worn path of corruption and bribery. A few, like Yeltsin, were incorruptible and took fresh initiatives to improve their local economies.

"Brezhnev . . . concerned himself with it [the country] less and less," according to Yeltsin. "The secretaries

███████████ The incompetence and senility
of the Soviet leadership of the 1970s and early
1980s is perfectly captured in this photograph.
Leonid Brezhnev and his political cronies view
1982 May Day celebrations from atop the Lenin
Mausoleum in Red Square. Brezhnev would
be dead of a heart attack within seven months.

of the Central Committee followed his example, so we found ourselves working completely on our own. We did receive occasional instructions, but they were pure eyewash, issued only for the record."[3]

This leads to the second reason why Yeltsin was left alone. He produced results. If he riled up the local apparatchiki a little, that could be overlooked, as long as he kept the region's economy on an even keel.

Yeltsin grew extremely skillful at taking advantage of Brezhnev in his dotage. He would visit Moscow on a Thursday, the last day of Brezhnev's workweek. The General Secretary was thinking about the weekend and anxious to get through with the week's business. One time, Yeltsin cajoled his leader into signing a paper that authorized the construction of a subway system for Sverdlovsk. Brezhnev took Yeltsin's dictation and signed the document without blinking an eye.

The ease with which Yeltsin got what he wanted out of the aging Brezhnev both pleased and distressed him. "How many of the rogues and cheats, indeed plain criminals, who surrounded Brezhnev exploited him for their own dishonest purposes?" he wondered. "How many resolutions or decrees did he calmly, unthinkingly sign, bringing riches to a few and suffering to many?"[4]

For all the good that Yeltsin was able to do in Sverdlovsk, the Soviet Union as a whole was in decay, rotting away under a system of privilege, bribes, and black marketeering. Yeltsin was beginning to see the need for reform on a national scale, but he was still, by his own admission, too inexperienced as a politician to do anything about it. When he did speak out at party congresses, he did so bluntly and undiplomatically, drawing more attention to his manner than his substance.

━━━━━━━━━━ The Brezhnev years
were marked by political corruption
and a failing Soviet economy. The
one meat available to shoppers in
this state-run meat market is sausage.

Another provincial first secretary, Mikhail Gorbachev, was more cautious and circumspect in his reform policies. Gorbachev and Yeltsin were similar in many ways, however. The two men were the same age, both came from the provinces, and both had fresh ideas and a certain charisma that they used to bring reform to their respective homelands—Yeltsin in Sverdlovsk and Gorbachev in Stavropol, a southern province near the Caucasus Mountains.

In other ways, Gorbachev and Yeltsin were very different. While Yeltsin came to the party late in life, Gorbachev got involved in politics while still a university student. He was a leader in the Komsomol, the youth branch of the Communist party, and was a full party member by the age of twenty-four. Gorbachev patiently worked his way up the political ladder to first secretary of Stavropol after years of political anonymity. He cultivated friendships with powerful men to further his career, most notably with Yuri Andropov, the head of the KGB, the Soviet secret police. Yeltsin, on the other hand, rose to first secretary very quickly. Yet he did little to curry favor with those who held influence. Indeed, he sometimes seemed to go out of his way to insult these very people who could help him the most.

Yeltsin and Gorbachev's paths first crossed in the mid-1970s. They struck a deal to exchange goods. Stavropol, known as one of the Soviet Union's breadbaskets, would give meat and bread to Sverdlovsk in exchange for lumber and steel. It was a good bartering system, one that brought the two party bosses into a political and personal friendship.

Gorbachev's subtle political maneuvering paid off handsomely in September 1978. Andropov saw to it that Brezhnev, on a train bound for the Far East on a diplomatic mission, stopped in Stavropol so Brezhnev could personally meet Andropov's protégé, Gorbachev. Yeltsin had also come out to meet Brezhnev's train at the Sverdlovsk platform. It sped by without stopping.

A few months later, Gorbachev was called to Moscow to become secretary of agriculture in the Secretariat of the Central Committee, a body of ten members who managed the day-to-day activities of the Communist party. At the same time, Yeltsin found himself in trouble with the Central Committee. Brezhnev, now in the final phase of his long career, was, like Stalin, turning his eyes to posterity. Memorials and statues of the great man were erected in towns and cities across the Soviet Union that were associated with his life and career. Brezhnev had gotten his first job as a land surveyor in Sverdlovsk, and Yeltsin was ordered by the Central Committee to turn the building where Brezhnev once worked into a museum.

Yeltsin, who had little real respect for his aging leader, ignored the directive. He asked with cutting sarcasm if the Central Committee wanted the baptismal font where Brezhnev was christened gold-plated, too. Yeltsin was immediately summoned to Moscow to explain his response. The man who questioned him was his old friend Gorbachev. His former colleague warned Yeltsin to watch his step in the future. This time he would get off with a warning, but to cross the Central Committee and its wishes again might have serious repercussions.

Despite this episode, Yeltsin maintained friendly relations with Gorbachev, and he periodically visited the secretary of agriculture to discuss farming problems in his province. Yeltsin recalled Gorbachev at that time as being "more open and frank" than he would later become.[5]

Their relationship deteriorated when Yeltsin received a critical report from Central Committee inspectors who visited Sverdlovsk. Yeltsin argued that the report they made on his performance was inaccurate. Again, Yeltsin stepped over the line of what was considered proper behavior for a party member. When he next met Gorbachev in Moscow, they had words. Yeltsin was gaining a reputation in Moscow as a troublemaker, a man who went out of his way to criticize his betters and draw attention to himself. This was not the way for a good apparatchik to get promoted.

On November 10, 1982, Brezhnev's long reign finally came to an end. He died suddenly at home from a heart attack. Yuri Andropov was elected his successor by the members of the Politburo, the fifteen-member policy-making body of the Communist party. Andropov saw the system needed reforming and started to enact changes, but he was a sick man. When he died a little over a year later, it looked like his top lieutenant, Gorbachev, would inherit the reins of power. But the Old Guard was not ready to allow a new generation to take over. They elected Konstantin Chernenko, an old Brezhnev crony and a loyal but unimaginative apparatchik, as the new Soviet leader. Chernenko, also plagued by ill-health, died about a year later.

Gorbachev's time had come. In March 1985 he was named the new leader of the Soviet Union. One month later, Boris Yeltsin received a call from Central Committee secretary Vladimir Dolgikh. He offered Yeltsin the job of head of the Central Committee's construction department. Yeltsin politely refused. Although he professed that he could better serve his country in Sverdlovsk, it is more likely that he wanted to come to Moscow as a member of the Central Committee, as his two predecessors had.

Yeltsin received a second call from one of Gorbachev's top deputies, Yegor Ligachev. Ligachev had been first secretary of the Siberian province of Tomsk; like Yeltsin, he had a reputation as an incorruptible and reform-minded party boss. He admired Yeltsin's drive and had been largely responsible for his invitation to Moscow. Ligachev repeated the invitation to Yeltsin, who realized he could not refuse a second time and continue his career in politics. He might be headstrong but he still had ambition and knew he could only go so far in asserting his independence.

In July 1985 the Yeltsins, their two daughters and their husbands, moved to Moscow. The maverick of the provinces was coming to the center of power. It would seem that with the reform-minded Gorbachev running the nation, Yeltsin's time had come.

CHAPTER FIVE

GORBACHEV'S BROOM

By 1986, Gorbachev was slowly beginning a program of reforms that would forever change the Soviet Union as it had existed for nearly seventy years. His economic policy of *perestroika*, meaning "restructuring" in Russian, would move the Soviet economy toward the kind of free market economy that the Western nations enjoyed. His policy of *glasnost*, a Russian word for "openness," lifted censorship of newspapers, books, and other mass media and allowed Soviets to look honestly at their past for the first time. Gorbachev needed trustworthy, forward-looking men he could count on to carry out the reforms necessary to improve the country. He felt that Yeltsin was one of these men.

Soon after his arrival, Gorbachev had Yeltsin elected a secretary of the Central Committee. He would later become a member of the prestigious Politburo. As a member of this privileged "club," Yeltsin was offered Gorbachev's old dacha, or country house. From an apartment with three rooms, the Yeltsins moved into a house that had its own movie theater. It was enough to make this man of the people squirm.

▬▬▬▬▬▬▬ This official photograph was
taken in 1986, after Boris Yeltsin came to
Moscow and was appointed Moscow party
boss by Soviet President Mikhail Gorbachev.

It was clear that Gorbachev was grooming Yeltsin for more than the job of construction head. In December he offered him the position of Moscow first party secretary, a job comparable to the mayor of an American city. Yeltsin again hesitated, but it was an opportunity he could not turn down. Gorbachev convinced him, he later wrote, that the "Moscow party organization was in need of a rescue operation."[1]

Moscow did indeed need to be rescued—largely from its politicians. One of Europe's greatest cities, Moscow had been run for decades by corrupt and inept party bureaucrats who had made it their private kingdom. Viktor Grishin, who Yeltsin replaced as first secretary, was a totally corrupt politician and one of Gorbachev's chief rivals for party leadership before Chernenko's death. Vladimir Promyslov, another city leader, had been the official mayor of Moscow for twenty-two years. He spent much of his time away from the capital on trips abroad. A standing joke among Muscovites was that Promyslov once stopped over in Moscow on the way from Washington, D.C., to Tokyo.

Through the neglect and corruption of Grishin, Promsyslov, and others, Moscow had become a city without direction. It was dirty, overcrowded, and lacking in the kind of cultural richness that made Leningrad the jewel of Russia. Out of a population of over 8.5 million people, more than a third were in need of an apartment. Meanwhile 5 million visitors a year filled hotels and hostels to bursting.

Gorbachev knew that his reforms had to start in the capital. He had faith that Yeltsin would not let him down. The man from Sverdlovsk would prove the truthfulness of an old Russian proverb all too well—"A new broom sweeps clean."[2]

When Yeltsin became party
boss of Moscow, the Soviet capital was dirty,
overcrowded, and riddled with corruption.
These Muscovites are rushing by one of the
city's largest department stores.

Yeltsin wasted no time in going to work. He replaced twenty-three out of thirty-three district party secretaries in Moscow. When some of his new appointments proved to be no better than their predecessors, he dismissed them, too. He got rid of 40 percent of party functionaries in the City Committee and 36 percent of the city bureaucrats.

To set a good example for the incoming officials, Yeltsin practiced the self-sacrifice and commitment he so fervently preached. He did without the black limousines favored by party bosses and rode to work on city buses and subways. He listened as commuters complained about the inefficiency of the city's transportation system. He visited factories and stores, often unannounced, to see how workers and consumers were treated. In the moments before he was recognized, Yeltsin could see for himself who was guilty of mismanagement.

In public places he held what would become his trademark—long, exhaustive press conferences. Soviet officials in general avoided the public spotlight. When they did give a press conference, it was carefully controlled. This changed as Gorbachev's policy of glasnost took hold, but it was a gradual process that many bureaucrats felt uncomfortable with.

This was not true of Yeltsin. He relished every opportunity to hear what was on the people's minds and then tell them what was on his own. Any question was permissible, no matter how personal or potentially embarrassing. He wouldn't leave until the last question was answered, which made for marathon conferences often lasting four or five hours.

Yeltsin was quick to admit the failure of politicians to meet the needs of the people. "Muscovites—

workers in particular—are straightforward folk," he wrote. "They call a spade a spade. And sometimes I feel ashamed and embarrassed in front of them because we officials could have done more, but we haven't."[3]

Yeltsin's efforts to do more were often frustrated by the city's entrenched bureaucracy. In Sverdlovsk, Yeltsin had been in total command of his domain. He could cut through the red tape and usually get his way. Life was much more complicated in Moscow. The city had layer upon layer of bureaucracy, and Yeltsin, a stranger to the big city and its ways, was often overwhelmed by it. It didn't help that his fiery temperament made political compromise almost impossible. He was impatient, explosive, and always combative. Still, people loved him for going up against the bureaucracy in their name, despite his high rate of failure.

As an example, Yeltsin tried to put a ban on *limitchiki*, workers without permanent residence in Moscow, who were taking jobs away from Muscovites by working for lower wages. Managers and employers resisted Yeltsin's plan, and eventually he was overruled by the Central Committee.

If Yeltsin could not change the core of the city, he did what he could to improve its surface. He added more bus routes to help commuters and ease the transportation problem. He replaced old factories in central Moscow with shops, restaurants, museums, and theaters. He gave the people a place to find moderately priced entertainment and cultural activities, while at the same time cutting down on the city's air pollution from industry. He found a way to get fresh fruits and vegetables into Moscow's markets from other republics by cutting out middlemen. He organized police raids to crack down on crime rings dealings in drugs, prostitution, and the black market.

However, for every petty thief or small-time drug peddler that Yeltsin's police caught, there was a bigger crook that went free. Crime and corruption were too entrenched in the Communist system to root them out. Yeltsin was beginning to realize that these ills weren't afflicting the Communist system of government; they were symptoms of the system itself. This was a diagnosis that Gorbachev, for all his talk about *perestroika*, wasn't prepared to make. In an interview with a Yugoslav magazine in October 1986, Yeltsin spoke out with characteristic bluntness: "An economic reform does not yield benefits if it stops halfway, if it comes down to a compromise, to an attempt to paint the car instead of replacing the worn-out engine."

Muscovites respected and loved Yeltsin and saw him as the one politician who was on their side. They invented a new unit of measurement—a *yelt*—to measure progress in Gorbachev's reforms. Such praise was given at the expense of Gorbachev, whose record for change fell below Yeltsin's high standards. Although Gorbachev was seen as a charismatic leader in the United States and Western Europe, at home he was seen as a clever politician, something of a patrician, and a man of the status quo.

Yeltsin's outspokenness about the slow pace of reform began to irk his mentor. Gorbachev had looked to Yeltsin as both an ally and something of a political tool to keep the agenda moving forward and take some of the heat from the conservative right off himself. But now Yeltsin's reputation as a reformer in Moscow and as a critic in the Politburo was outshining his own. For the sake of his own position, Gorbachev now agreed with many of his more conservative rivals that Yeltsin needed to be brought down a few pegs. In May 1987, Yeltsin gave the party the ammunition it had been looking for.

Pamyat, which means "memory" in Russian, was an organization of Russian nationalists who were pro-*perestroika* and anti-Communist. They were also anti-Semitic and anti-foreigner. On May 6, radical members of Pamyat gathered to demonstrate in Manezh Square near the Kremlin. They refused to disperse until they met with Gorbachev and Yeltsin. Impulsively, Yeltsin agreed to meet with the protesters. He spoke with them for two hours. He told them: "Many say bad things about you. But you provoke this with your remarks verging on anti-Sovietism. We will consider recognizing you—but only as a truly patriotic organization."[4]

The incident called Yeltsin's own patriotism into question, and he was unfairly accused of supporting Pamyat's radical, aggressive nationalism. Instead of admitting he had made a mistake by meeting personally with the radicals, Yeltsin pigheadedly struck back. "If the demonstrators had gotten a few blows on the head with clubs, that would have appeased my opponents," he said.[5] But the issue was as much about Yeltsin's judgment as a leader as it was about the politics of Pamyat.

The ferocity of the criticism stung and further alienated him from his colleagues in the Politburo. When he brought the same reforming fervor from the streets of Moscow to the meetings of the Politburo, Yeltsin found himself alone, with no support from Gorbachev. "I could never rid myself of the feeling that I was an outsider—or rather, an alien—among these people;

that somehow I didn't belong within the framework of a set of ideas that I found incomprehensible. . . . I would express my views fairly, sharply, frankly, and directly," he later wrote. "To be honest, my remarks had little effect, but they profoundly disturbed the placid atmosphere of the sessions."[6]

"Gorbachev's broom" was stirring up trouble for the very man who had first set it in motion. Yeltsin sensed his days in the Politburo were numbered and decided that it was wiser to step down before he was thrown out. On September 12, 1987, he wrote a letter to Gorbachev, who was vacationing on the Black Sea. "I am ill-equipped to work at the Politburo . . ." he explained. "I am aware that I am causing problems."[7] Yeltsin requested that Gorbachev release him of his duties as first secretary of the Moscow party committee.

Gorbachev was slow to respond. While Yeltsin waited tensely for a reply, he attended a reunion of alumni of the Ural Polytechnical Institute. He confided to his friends from his college days: "Another year and a half, two years like this—and you'll see my obituary in the papers."[8] In fact, Yeltsin's political downfall was only a few short months away.

CHAPTER SIX

ODD MAN OUT

The seventieth anniversary of the Russian Revolution was a historic occasion for the Soviet party leadership, but not one without its problems. On the one hand, Gorbachev wanted to use the October Revolution as a means of legitimizing his own reform movement as part of a great Soviet tradition. On the other hand, the dismal conditions that had led to Gorbachev's reforms were a direct result of decades of the abuse of power under Stalin and his Communist heirs. Gorbachev had prepared a speech to give comfort to the traditionalists in the party and at the same time give hope to those who yearned for change.

On October 21, 1987, the Central Committee met behind closed doors to hear Gorbachev deliver the rough draft of the speech he would present a few weeks later to the public. When Gorbachev finished, Yegor Ligachev, who chaired the meeting, asked for comments from the committee members. Liberals and conservatives alike said nothing. None of them wanted to rock Gorbachev's ship of state, at least not in such an official meeting. But there was one man who could hold his silence no longer. Boris Yeltsin asked to speak. Gorbachev hesitated, perhaps sensing what was to come. Then he gave Yeltsin permission to address the committee.

Clearly nervous, Yeltsin mounted the rostrum. He spoke for about four minutes, with only a few notes. In those four minutes he shook the very foundation of the Soviet state. Unsure of himself and sometimes stumbling over his words, Yeltsin unleashed a personal attack on the number two man in the government, Ligachev. He accused him of deliberately sabotaging Gorbachev's reforms in Moscow. Ligachev, who had helped bring Yeltsin to Moscow, had little in common with him politically. Ligachev was a conservative who accepted reform of the Communist system, but believed fervently that that system had to remain in place. He and Yeltsin had been in serious disagreement in one Politburo meeting after another.

Yeltsin went on to criticize the very policy of *perestroika* itself, arguing that it was moving too slowly. While change was on the lips of every politician, little change had actually taken place. Indeed, Yeltsin declared, reform had come to a standstill. Finally, Yeltsin did the unthinkable. He attacked Gorbachev himself, claiming his fellow Politburo members had created a "cult of personality" around their leader that was counterproductive and dangerous. He ended by announcing his resignation from both the Moscow party leadership and the Politburo, saying he could no longer work in such a system.

When Yeltsin finished speaking the great hall was silent. A dreadful pall had fallen over it. Yeltsin returned to his seat. "My heart was pounding and seemed ready to burst through my rib cage," he later wrote in his autobiography. "I knew what would happen next. I would be slaughtered in an organized, methodical manner, and the job would be done almost with pleasure and enjoyment."[1]

Yeltsin was not mistaken. Gorbachev, clearly furious with his protégé, opened the floor for responses to his speech. Ligachev, who had borne the brunt of Yeltsin's criticism, launched the first salvo. He defended himself, claiming to be shocked at Yeltsin's assault. He took Yeltsin to task for attacking *perestroika* and casting "doubt on our whole policy."[2] Other Central Committee members were quick to join in the chorus of disapproval. "I have been in the Central Committee for twenty-six years," said Sergei Manuakin, chairman of the People's Control Committee. "Never have I heard such a speech. . . . This has happened because of the political immaturity of Comrade Yeltsin."[3]

Yeltsin was not surprised by the ferocity of those he considered his enemies. What surprised and hurt him was when people he thought were his friends joined in the attack. They included Prime Minister Nikolai Ryzhkov, an old friend and worker from Sverdlovsk, and Minister of Foreign Affairs Eduard Shevardnadze, who privately shared many of Yeltsin's views. Yeltsin's speech, according to Shevardnadze, showed "irresponsibility in the face of the Party, the people, the friends and colleagues in the Politburo."[4]

Out of twenty-seven speakers, only Georgi Arbatov, director of the United States–Canada Research Institute, defended Yeltsin, but his defense was half-hearted at best. "You cannot deny his courage,"[5] Arbatov said, and he was promptly attacked by the next speaker for daring to defend Yeltsin.

Why had Yeltsin committed what surely was political suicide? ". . . how could I carry on?" he wrote in his autobiography. "I could, but I would have had to become a different person, to stop speaking my mind, not notice that the country was sliding into an abyss while at the same time proclaiming loudly that the party—organized and inspired, of course, by its general secretary—was the architect of *perestroika*."[6]

Gorbachev finally gave Yeltsin the opportunity to reply to his critics. Disheartened and unnerved, Yeltsin backed off. He realized that he had gone too far and that unless he tempered his criticism he would face political exile or worse. He qualified what he had said and asserted that only one or two members of the Politburo had been guilty of spreading Gorbachev's "cult of personality." But it was too late for a retraction. Gorbachev's policies had been harshly attacked, not by the right, which he was used to, but by a man more liberal than himself. The charges stung, and Gorbachev struck back, using the very criticism that Yeltsin had leveled against him. "Isn't it enough for you that all Moscow revolves around your person?" Gorbachev retorted. "Do you need the Central Committee to bother itself about you as well?"[7]

This attack on Yeltsin, the grandstander, was one that struck a chord with many men in the room. In their view, Yeltsin had been shooting off his big mouth ever since he arrived in Moscow. He had made a name for himself in the media by going into factories and schools, getting his picture in the papers, and holding his interminable press conferences. Never mind that Gorbachev had used some of these same methods to get his message out. Yeltsin always went too far. In the eyes of many, he was an adventurer and a political opportunist who needed his comeuppance.

Under the barrage of attacks, Yeltsin was backed into a corner and saw no way of getting out, except by admitting defeat. "By letting down the Central Committee and the Moscow city organization in my speech today, I made a mistake," he confessed.[8]

The "Yeltsin affair," as it came to be called, was kept quiet by the main principals involved, although word of what had taken place in the committee meeting soon leaked out to the press. Gorbachev made no immediate move to act on Yeltsin's resignation, and Yeltsin went about his daily business, waiting for the axe to fall.

At the seventieth anniversary Yeltsin joined the other Soviet officials atop Lenin's Mausoleum in Red Square, the traditional viewing stand for all parades and celebrations in Moscow. None of his colleagues dared to approach Yeltsin, but two foreigners were not afraid to show him their support. Cuban leader Fidel Castro hugged him warmly. So did Polish president Wojciech Jaruzelski, who in Russian encouraged him to "hang in there, Boris!"[9]

But the events of the past two weeks had taken their toll on the man whose nickname was "the Bulldozer." Two days after the anniversary Yeltsin was hospitalized with severe headaches and chest pains. In truth, he had suffered a complete nervous breakdown. He was monitored by intravenous procedure, and his condition was considered serious enough to keep all visitors away, including his wife.

On November 11 the phone by Yeltsin's bed rang. It was Gorbachev, summoning him to a Moscow party committee meeting at once. Yeltsin couldn't believe his ears. But Gorbachev was dead serious, and Yeltsin knew it would be unwise to ignore the summons. While doctors pumped him up with tranquilizers to get him on his feet, Naina berated the KGB (state security) colonel sent to fetch him. "Your job is to take care of him, and now you're killing him with your cowardice!" she ranted.[10]

Yeltsin arrived at the assembly meeting feeling groggy and disoriented. This meeting was not held behind closed doors. Gorbachev made sure the television cameras were there to record the humiliation of Boris Yeltsin. Again, personal attacks were made against Yeltsin by twenty-four of his colleagues. For four hours, Yeltsin listened, although in his dazed condition he probably didn't hear all that was said. "His lips were purple," recalled one eyewitness. "He was all blue, and he had difficulty keeping his head up."[11]

When it was over, Yeltsin stumbled up to the rostrum. A broken, sick man, his words at times were almost incoherent. His speech bore a disturbing resemblance to the speeches of the victims of Stalin's "show trials" of the 1930s, who had been coached and rehearsed in their "confessions."

"I am guilty before the Moscow city party organization, Moscow City Party Committee, before you, and, of course, I am very guilty before Mikhail Sergeyevich Gorbachev," he said.[12]

Yeltsin was stripped of his position as first Moscow secretary, although he was left his position on the Politburo for the time being. When the meeting ended, Gorbachev helped the ailing Yeltsin out of the hall and waited with him in Yeltsin's old office for an ambulance to take him back to the hospital.

Shortly after, Gorbachev offered Yeltsin a new job as first deputy chairman of the State Committee for Construction in Gosstroi. It was a big demotion. The man who ran Moscow would be back in the building

Originally allies and friends, Yeltsin and Gorbachev turned into political enemies as Yeltsin became a more and more outspoken critic of Gorbachev's failing policies.

trade he had left fifteen years earlier. Yeltsin accepted the job. It wasn't much, but it was work. He turned down an alternative offer of early retirement, knowing that a few months in a rocking chair would be the death of him.

The public career of Boris Yeltsin, at age fifty-six, seemed all but over. But if Gorbachev thought he had settled the "Yeltsin affair," he was very mistaken. The people of Moscow, Sverdlovsk, and other cities were appalled by Yeltsin's confession and his swift fall from power. What had he said in the speech on October 21 that was so terrible it could bring his political career to such an abrupt end?

People were left to imagine what the speech contained. They imagined Yeltsin had called for everything from the early withdrawal of troops from Afghanistan to the downfall of communism. Students at Moscow State University held a rally and demanded that the Kremlin publish Yeltsin's speech. In a forum in a liberal Moscow magazine, thousands of readers demanded to know why the speech had not been released and why Yeltsin had been punished. Demonstrations and riots followed in cities around the country, including Leningrad and Sverdlovsk.

The speech began to take on a life of its own, apart from the reality of what Yeltsin had actually said at the assembly meeting. It became a symbol of the expectations of the country's people and the failure of Gorbachev's policies to live up to them. "It doesn't matter so much whether Yeltsin said these things," wrote Soviet intellectual Lev Timofeyev. "What matters is that Soviets want someone to have said them."[13]

Different versions of the speech, none of them entirely accurate, began to circulate around the country and abroad. When Gorbachev realized his mistake and had the speech published in the spring of 1989, the public was disappointed that Yeltsin hadn't gone further in his attack on the government.

Gorbachev's plan to discredit his rival had backfired. Rather than make him a scapegoat, Gorbachev had turned Yeltsin into a folk hero. At the same time, he had made himself and his government look all the more a failure.

Yeltsin's new job in Gosstroi was hateful to him. He was stuck behind a desk shuffling papers when he wanted to be out among the people. His health began to deteriorate again. He took out his frustration on his family and closest friends. He described his state of mind in his autobiography: "All that was left where my heart had been was a burned-out cinder. Everything around me was burned out, everything within me was burned out."[14]

In the next year and a half, Yeltsin saw Gorbachev only once. Other officials and colleagues acknowledged him at meetings but cautiously kept their distance. "Politically I didn't exist. . . . I was a corpse," he recalled.[15]

But the real corpse was the Soviet state, which was rotting from decades of mismanagement and corruption. Yeltsin's dramatic fall from power sent a message to the people that an honest and forthright man could no longer work in this decadent system. As Vladimir Solovyov and Elena Klepikova perceptively noted, "Yeltsin's fall, like that of the stone that looses an avalanche, led to the chain reaction of cataclysms within Soviet society."[16]

The odd man out of that society was about to find a way back in.

CHAPTER SEVEN

A NEW DAY

"In Stalin's time, ex-politicians were shot," wrote Yeltsin in his autobiography. "Khrushchev pensioned them off; in Brezhnev's 'era of stagnation,' they were packed off as ambassadors to distant countries. Here, too, Gorbachev's *perestroika* had set a new precedent: a dismissed politician is now given the opportunity of returning to political life."[1]

Not that Gorbachev wanted Yeltsin back in circulation, but he could hardly force him out of the game entirely. This would only reflect badly on his own reform policies, and Yeltsin had created enough damage there already.

So Yeltsin was allowed to speak out again, granting interviews to foreign journalists and a few Soviet ones. He was frank about the events that had led to his fall from grace. "A fight is always a fight," he told one Western reporter. "You attack, you go on the defensive, and sometimes you get knocked down."[2]

To show that he was back on his feet again, Yeltsin attended the 19th Party Conference in the Kremlin on June 28, 1988. Gorbachev did what he could to keep

Yeltsin away by pressuring the Sverdlovsk local party committee to deny Yeltsin a delegate's seat. Finally, at the last minute, Yeltsin was nominated as a delegate to the conference from the Karelian Autonomous Republic on the border of Finland. It is possible that Gorbachev allowed this to avoid any controversy.

Yeltsin requested to speak to the 5,000 delegates, but his request was ignored. Finally on July 1, the last day of the conference, he decided to take matters into his own hands. Still suffering from poor health, Yeltsin rushed past KGB agents and reached the rostrum. He came face-to-face with Gorbachev. Yeltsin demanded that he be allowed to speak; if not, he would force a vote from the floor on the matter. Gorbachev tried some stalling tactics, but Yeltsin was resolute. Gorbachev saw no alternative but to let Yeltsin speak.

This time Yeltsin was tactful and well prepared. He opened with another attack on Ligachev, but this was acceptable, since Ligachev had fallen out with Gorbachev and was no longer a power to be reckoned with. He avoided any direct criticism of Gorbachev and ended his speech with a fervent plea on his own behalf. "Rehabilitation after fifty years has now become habitual. . . . But I am asking for political rehabilitation while I am still alive," he said.[3] The plea failed to stir the sympathies of the Kremlin leaders. Gorbachev took the podium and chastised Yeltsin again for his grandstanding. Then came the inevitable chorus of disapproval from the apparatchiki.

But something had happened since the last conference. The Soviet people, sympathetic from the start with Yeltsin and his plight, were now seriously questioning the Kremlin's motives in this latest confrontation. The growing wave of support for Yeltsin swept across much of the country. Thousands of letters flooded in backing the new man in the Ministry of Construction. Along with political advice, people sent him medical advice on how to get well. They even sent him honey and herbal remedies.

By November, Yeltsin felt strong enough to hold his own press conference, although he didn't call it that. He met with students of the Higher Komosol School in Moscow and answered their questions for four and a half hours. One student asked him: "You're no less popular in the country than Gorbachev. Could you lead the Party and the State?" Replied Yeltsin: "When we have alternative elections—why not give it a try?"[4]

Yeltsin would soon have a chance to do just that. As part of his reform movement, Gorbachev announced the first democratic election to be held in the Soviet Union in seventy years. The Soviet people were to elect 2,250 People's Deputies for a special Congress that would help determine the country's future. On December 13, 1988, Yeltsin announced that he would run in the election.

Yeltsin decided to run as a deputy from Moscow, to prove he was still well loved by the people of that city. The Kremlin did everything in its power to discredit Yeltsin before the election. They paid men to write threatening graffiti on the door of his apartment. They printed slanders against him in the press. Then two weeks before the March 1989 election, the Kremlin released to the press the transcript of Yeltsin's infamous speech of October 21, 1987, before the Central Committee. They thought it would discredit Yeltsin, but the speech only further enhanced his reputation as a steadfast reformer and a man of integrity.

In the election, Yeltsin won 89.6 percent of all the

votes cast in Moscow, defeating the official party candidate in a landslide. Yeltsin had defied the state and won. He was no longer simply a thorn in Gorbachev's side but a dangerous political rival. The two met for an hour after the election. Gorbachev asked Yeltsin what his future plans were. Yeltsin was evasive. He turned down several positions that Gorbachev offered him. It was growing increasingly clear to Gorbachev that Yeltsin was after his job.

The next election to be held was for the Supreme Soviet. This permanent governing body of 542 deputies would be elected from and by the Congress of Deputies. Yeltsin ran on a slate of a dozen candidates competing for eleven seats. He ended up as the only one of the twelve that didn't get elected. The Kremlin political machine had worked overtime to keep Yeltsin out of power.

At the last minute, however, pressure from the public and liberals led Yuri Kazannik, a liberal deputy from Omsk, to concede his seat to Yeltsin. "What should I say to my voters?" Kazannik told Yeltsin. "They know there's six million Muscovites behind you. If I stay, my voters will kill me."[5]

Soon after, the Supreme Soviet met for the first time in televised hearings. Something very unexpected happened. Yeltsin, instead of being the odd man out this time, became a role model. Hundreds of delegates became "little Yeltsins," speaking out against every imaginable abuse of the state. The Soviet people sat glued to their televisions at the remarkable sight of Communist party members criticizing their own government. Many of these diatribes were pure grandstanding, giving each politician, no matter how minor his position, a moment in the spotlight. But despite the

Yeltsin savors his victory after winning a seat in the Supreme Soviet in May 1989. Less than a year before, many people thought his political career was over.

excesses, it was a historic occasion. "It was as though the entire nation. . . .woke up from hibernation," wrote Yeltsin.[6]

Yeltsin, along with dissident physicist Andrei Sakharov, became one of the leaders in the Supreme Soviet. In July the deputies founded an Interregional Group with five leaders, two of whom were Yeltsin and Sakharov. Yeltsin became the first rotating leader of the 362-member group.

The first two democratic elections in the Soviet Union had brought Yeltsin back from obscurity to national prominence, but he could not yet compete with Gorbachev on the larger stage of international affairs. Much of Gorbachev's reputation rested on his summit meetings with U.S. President Ronald Reagan and other European leaders that helped reduce the arms race and end the Cold War. Yeltsin, in contrast, had only been abroad four times—twice to Germany and once each to Cuba and Nicaragua. He decided the time had come to broaden his horizons and gain some experience as a spokesperson for the Opposition. The Kremlin was not anxious to see Yeltsin go abroad. The government denied him a travel permit to go to West Germany to participate in a discussion on East-West relations.

Yeltsin next applied to visit the United States, a country he greatly admired for its democratic traditions and its economical success. The government allowed Yeltsin to make the trip, knowing he would first have to find a sponsor in the United States. The Kremlin felt confident that no major American organization would risk offending Gorbachev by sponsoring the visit of his political rival. But James Harrison of the Esalen Institute was not afraid, and he agreed to sponsor Yeltsin.

Yeltsin's trip was to be two weeks long, but the Central Committee cut it back to one week. He visited nine states and eleven cities, giving speeches at various universities on the future of his country. Personally, it was a richly rewarding experience for Yeltsin, but publicly, it had mixed results. Harrison called Yeltsin's visit "a sensation" that brought him to the attention of the American public.[7] Others, however, found Yeltsin in his meetings with American reporters and politicians to be as clumsy and oafish as the proverbial Russian bear. Unfounded rumors spread that Yeltsin was spending most of his time off the lecture platform drinking, eating, and buying up video equipment and cassettes with his lecture fees.

In fact, Yeltsin's exposure to the wealth of consumer goods in the United States left him deeply depressed. He wrote:

> When I saw those [supermarket] shelves crammed with hundreds, thousands of cans, cartons, and goods of every possible sort, for the first time I felt quite fairly sick with despair for the Soviet People. That such a potentially superrich country as ours has been brought to a state of such poverty! It is terrible to think of it.[8]

Although he was not officially recognized as the head of the Opposition in his country, Yeltsin still had hopes that a meeting with U.S. President George Bush would help to legitimize his position. Bush, however, was a firm Gorbachev supporter and was reluctant to meet with Yeltsin. On the fourth day of his trip, Yeltsin was driven by limousine to the White House. When he was told he would not be meeting with Bush but National Security Advisor Brent Scowcroft, Yeltsin refused to leave his limo. It was finally agreed that Bush would drop by to see Yeltsin at Scowcroft's office. Yeltsin accepted this compromise and got out of the car.

Bush was good to his word and spent fifteen minutes chatting with Yeltsin. When asked by reporters for his impression of the Soviet visitor, Bush said he found Yeltsin to be "a jolly fellow."[9]

The *Washington Post* was even more condescending in a feature story subtitled "Yeltsin's Boozy Bearhug for the Capitalists." Yeltsin attributed some of his grogginess at the lectern not to alcohol but a lack of sleep, jet lag, and medication. The Kremlin kept the drunkenness rumors alive by slowing down the speed of a tape of a speech he delivered at Johns Hopkins University to make his words appear slurred.

When Yeltsin returned to the Soviet Union on September 18, *Pravda*, the official Soviet newspaper, was quick to print the report of an Italian journalist who followed Yeltsin's U.S. tour. According to the journalist, "He [Yeltsin] now has everything he dreamed about: whiskey, dollars, knickknacks, and *Rambo* videocassettes."[10]

Yeltsin called the article "hogwash" and pointed out that all of the $100,000 in lecture fees he earned went to buying disposable syringes to combat the spread of AIDS in the Soviet Union. But the Kremlin slander machine had only started. It soon added more serious dirty tricks to its campaign to discredit Yeltsin.

On September 29, Moscow police were surprised when a drenched-to-the-skin Boris Yeltsin walked into their headquarters. Yeltsin explained that he had been abducted by four men in the street who put a bag over his head, drove him to a nearby bridge, and pushed him into the Moscow River. Embarrassed by the incident, he asked the police not to file an official report. Yeltsin drank tea while his clothes dried out and waited for his wife to pick him up.

The Kremlin quickly spread rumors that Yeltsin had other reasons for not letting the report be filed. One rumor claimed that he had been visiting a mistress when her husband arrived home and threw him into the river. Another rumor said that the mistress dumped a bucket of water over him.

The truth remains elusive. Even in his autobiography, Yeltsin skirts the issue while calling the rumors "obvious nonsense."[11] By most reliable accounts, it appears he was returning from a visit to an old friend, Prime Minister Nikolai Ryzhkov, when he was accosted by the men, probably government agents.

The Kremlin had done everything in its power to tarnish Yeltsin's reputation with the Soviet people. But he remained more popular than ever. On December 14, 1989, Andrei Sakharov, age sixty-eight, died. Boris Yeltsin was now the unchallenged voice of conscience in the Soviet Union.

CHAPTER EIGHT

THE CENTER
FALLS APART

In the five years since Mikhail Gorbachev had come to power, his reforms had weakened and damaged a Communist system that most Soviets found antiquated, repressive, and unjust.

As the Soviet Union turned its attention to problems at home, it withdrew troops and influence from the governments of Eastern Europe that it had previously dominated. These countries began their own internal struggle for freedom from communism. The first to elect a free, non-Communist government was Poland in 1989. Czechoslovakia, Hungary, and other countries would soon follow.

The Kremlin accepted these changes, but when one of its own republics started rumbling for independence, the reaction was very different. Tiny Lithuania was one of the three Baltic states on the western edge of the Soviet Union. Unlike the other two, Latvia and Estonia, Lithuania had been a free country centuries before it was first annexed by Russia at the end of the nineteenth century.

If Lithuania was allowed its freedom, Gorbachev

reasoned, how many other of the USSR's fifteen republics would ask to be free? In his mind, Gorbachev, for all his progressive thinking, could no more envision the breakup of the Soviet Union than he could the collapse of communism. He imposed an economic blockade on Lithuania to squelch the independence movement. It did little to enhance the reputation of the man who preached democratic change and *glasnost*.

On May 1, 1990, the traditional May Day festivities in Red Square were disrupted by liberal demonstrators who carried placards reading "Free Lithuania Now!" Gorbachev and other leaders left the reviewing stand to taunting chants of "Shame! Shame!" from a crowd below.

Yeltsin, not surprisingly, supported freedom for Lithuania. "If people have set their heart on self-determination, you cannot hold them back," he said in one speech.[1] He was not only thinking of Lithuania when he spoke those words. In Yeltsin's eyes, Russia, itself, the biggest and richest republic of the Soviet Union, should be independent and free from the control of the Kremlin. It was a radical idea, but one that people were beginning to consider as their frustration with Gorbachev and his policies mounted.

Later that month, Yeltsin entered the race for the chairmanship of the Russian Supreme Council. The position traditionally held little real power, but in Yeltsin's hands it could be used to promote his idea of Russian independence. Gorbachev realized what Yeltsin might do with this position and did everything he could to block Yeltsin's election. The voting went through three grueling rounds with Yeltsin beating the party candidate by 32 votes. One of Chairman Yeltsin's first acts was to meet with Lithuanian President

Vytautas Landsbergis. He promised full cooperation with Lithuania and helped to end the economic blockade that had crippled the tiny republic.

In July 1990, the 28th Congress of the Communist party convened in Moscow. It was an event that seemed more and more irrelevant to the Soviet people. This time, when Boris Yeltsin rose to the podium it was to make a very brief and dramatic statement. He declared his resignation from the Communist party and walked out of the hall. Such an act a few years ago would have been political suicide. But in 1990, Yeltsin had no more need of the party. It was the party that now needed him.

Soon after, Yeltsin left on a 22-day working tour of all Russia, the kind of punishing fact-finding mission he had undertaken so often in the past. He crossed ten time zones and visited seven republics and regions. When he returned home he told the press: "I saw too many tears and heard too many people talk—it will stay in my soul for many years. I will not rest till we put this mess in order."[2]

President Gorbachev was reacting to "this mess" in his country in a very different manner. His course of moderation between leftists and rightists was no longer tenable. Political maneuvering, no matter how well intended, would not solve the growing economic problems of the country. They called for bold and decisive actions, which Gorbachev seemed reluctant, or unable, to carry out. The people blamed him increasingly for their troubles. In one magazine poll the question was: "Who do you trust the most?" Yeltsin received 1,420 votes, Gorbachev, 115.

Unable or unwilling to push through more radical measures to stimulate the economy, Gorbachev faced two choices. He could allow things to unravel further, or he could assume strong executive powers to keep order until the situation improved. Many of the people around him urged him to follow the latter course before the country faced a crisis that would bring it to the brink of anarchy.

As the Russian fall turned to bitter winter, Gorbachev reversed direction and moved to the right. He fired the most liberal member of his government, Minister of the Interior Vadim Bakatin. He clamped down censorship on newspapers and magazines. Foreign Minister Eduard Shevardnadze, another shining light in the Gorbachev cabinet, was so discouraged by the course of events that he resigned his position on New Year's Eve. Gorbachev replaced these men and others with conservatives, men he had formerly considered his enemies.

The year 1991 got off to a chilling start when Soviet troops opened fire on peaceful demonstrators in Vilnius, the capital of Lithuania, killing fifteen people. On February 1, Gorbachev announced a state of emergency in Lithuania. Yeltsin was disgusted. He went on Soviet television and delivered a 40-minute speech denouncing Gorbachev and his policies. It was his harshest criticism yet of the Soviet leader:

> . . . he paid lip service to the notion of perestroika, but in fact acted to preserve the system, maintain rigid central power, and keep autonomy away from the Republics—most of all, from Russia. . . . I disassociate myself from the President's position and his policies and I call for his immediate resignation. . . . I believe in Russia and I call on you, my esteemed fellow

citizens, fellow Russians, to believe in our Russia as well. I have made my choice, and now each of you must make his choice. . . .[3]

The choice that Yeltsin made was one he had been considering for a long time—independence for Russia. If Gorbachev wouldn't change, the Russian republic would move forward without him and the Soviet Union. Independence would free Russia from the fourteen smaller republics that in the past had drained it of its rich resources and given little back in return. Russia could better become a free and open democracy without the cumbersome bureaucracy of the Kremlin telling it what to do. In the spring, the Russian parliament adopted a Declaration of State Sovereignty that made it largely independent of the Soviet Union, in theory if not yet in reality.

A direct election for a new Russian president was set for June 12. There were six candidates, but only one of them had the general support of the people. Boris Yeltsin won with 60 percent of the vote.

It was a crowning triumph for the sixty-year-old politician from the provinces. After being hounded, scorned, and exiled by his peers, Yeltsin had become the legitimate leader of his people. He wasted no time in setting up a second trip to the country where he had previously been considered little more than a clown— the United States. President Bush made time for him. The Bush administration was still backing Gorbachev, but it realized that the time might come when Yeltsin eclipsed his rival.

Returning home, Yeltsin called for nothing less than a "rebirth of Russia."[4] He believed that his homeland had the people and resources to make it the

━━━━━━━━ Yeltsin leaves the voting booth before casting his vote for the first democratically elected president of the Russian Republic in June 1991. He won easily with 60 percent of the vote.

▬▬▬▬▬ American President George
Bush greets newly elected Russian President
Boris Yeltsin during a summit meeting at the
Kremlin on July 30, 1991. Soviet President
Mikhail Gorbachev looks on. The coup and
the transfer of power from Gorbachev to
Yeltsin are only weeks away.

greatest nation in Europe. But to achieve this goal, it had to build a strong economy that could feed, clothe, and house its people, while providing them with decent jobs and a comfortable standard of living. A free market economy based on competition was the answer. To achieve it, Yeltsin advocated reforming the Soviet tax policy, persuading large businesses to come under Russian jurisdiction, and creating private farms to grow bigger and better crops.

At the beginning of the year Yeltsin had predicted that 1991 "will be the year of decision: either democracy will be suffocated or we—democrats—will not merely survive but triumph."[5] These words would prove prophetic. On August 19, 1991, while Gorbachev took his annual vacation, five of the top men in his government began a coup to return the country to hard-line communism. For all their hatred of democratic change, these men were weak and vacillating. They were no match for the Russian people, led by their new president, who faced their tanks and soldiers with courage and determination.

In three days the coup had fizzled out. This last, desperate attempt to bring back the old ways was the death knell of communism. The Soviet Union was becoming a relic of the past. Gorbachev had been surpassed by the revolution that he had started. He now had to make way for a new leader, the hero of the failed coup—Boris Yeltsin.

CHAPTER NINE

YELTSIN TAKES CHARGE

After the coup of August 1991, the Soviet Union began to fall apart like a house of cards. Restless republics began to clamor for their independence from an antiquated state that was clearly dying. Ukraine was the first to declare its independence. It was quickly followed by Belarus, Moldova, Uzbekistan, and Kyrgyzstan.

Gorbachev did what he could to keep his crumbling empire together, but it was hopeless. Saved from being deposed by the coup, Gorbachev could not save himself from his unpopularity with the public and his own tarnished reputation. As for Yeltsin, his courageous stand in the coup made him the man of the hour. His popularity, long on the rise, soared to new heights. As the democratically elected president of Russia, he now had the mandate for change he had long sought.

Yeltsin seized the moment to make a bold move. He outlawed the Communist party. Disgusted with the hard-liners and their fumbled coup, the Russian people supported the ban. Yeltsin also assumed national control over important Russian resources such as oil and precious metals. He announced plans to lift price controls to move the country closer to a free market economy. He even raised the minimum wage, although prices continued to grow faster than wages.

As Yeltsin's executive powers expanded, Gorbachev's shrunk. Yeltsin got his long-awaited revenge on the man who had humiliated him many times in the past. He refused to fund the ministries of Gorbachev's office. Soon the realm of the president of the Soviet Union was reduced to his personal staff and bodyguards. The international press were beginning to call Gorbachev a leader without a country.

The dismantling of the Soviet Union accelerated at a pace that must have surprised even Yeltsin. On December 8, Russia, Belarus, and Ukraine signed the Minsk Agreement, which declared that the USSR ceased to exist as "a subject of international law and geopolitical reality."[1] Two weeks later, eleven former republics of the Soviet Union joined together to form the Commonwealth of Independent States (CIS) and pledged to work together as democratic republics on matters of the economy, the environment, and foreign policy. The only republics that declined to join the CIS were the Baltic states of Estonia, Latvia, and Lithuania, and Georgia.

On January 1, 1992, the Soviet Union was officially dissolved. Gorbachev resigned his office and became a private citizen. Boris Yeltsin, long the maverick of Soviet politics, suddenly found himself in charge.

Freedom, however, had its price. Age-old antagonisms between ethnic and religious groups had been erupting since Gorbachev had begun loosening the grip of Soviet power several years before. Azerbaijan and Armenia had gone to war over Armenians living in

Azerbaijan. The Georgian government fought with Muslim separatists who lived within its borders. Civil war erupted in Tadjikistan between pro-democrats and Communists.

Meanwhile, Yeltsin was doing everything he could to move the Russian economy forward. Where Gorbachev had pulled back from radical measures, looking for a safe consensus among politicians, Yeltsin fearlessly forged ahead, confident that his mandate from the people would protect him from the criticisms of his political rivals. He brought into his government forward-looking young men in their thirties and forties. They included economists who favored a free market economy and had bold ideas on how to make it work in Russia. With their expertise, Yeltsin hoped to achieve what Gorbachev had failed to do—successfully turn the authoritarian Soviet economy into a capitalistic, free market economy based on open competition.

While Yeltsin's popularity remained high at home, he did not cut as impressive a figure as his predecessor abroad. Anxious to disprove his boorish reputation in the United States, the new Yeltsin appeared stiff and formal in his meetings with foreign leaders. On his third visit to the United States, in June 1992, he had his first summit meeting with President Bush and addressed a joint meeting of Congress. After the summit, he toured Kansas and tried his hand at harvesting wheat. The warmth and charisma of the former Moscow party boss began to shine through in his encounters with local farmers and their families.

Back in Moscow, however, Yeltsin's reforms were beginning to come under attack. In early March, former Communists and ultranationalists held an anti-government demonstration. Yeltsin unwisely sent

police to break it up. In the violent clash that followed, twenty police officers and seven demonstrators were injured. By trying to break up the demonstration, Yeltsin only drew more attention to the antigovernment forces and their cause.

Those forces were growing daily, not only in the streets of Moscow but in the very institution where Yeltsin had once triumphed—the Russian parliament. The 1,030-member parliament had been elected in 1989, more than two years before the downfall of the Communist party and the Soviet Union. Many of its members were still die-hard Communists who resented their loss of privileges and felt that Yeltsin's reforms would ruin the country. Other members of parliament were nationalists, fearful of their country's falling status among the world's nations. These two groups, which would seem to have little in common, formed an alliance to bring down Yeltsin and change the direction of Russia's future.

Chief among Yeltsin's political rivals was the speaker of parliament, Ruslan Khasbulatov, whose undisguised contempt for the Russian president was even greater than Yeltsin's contempt had been for Gorbachev. Khasbulatov's strongest ally in parliament was

■■■■■■ **Yeltsin has always been a fierce competitor in sports as well as politics. A soccer star in college, he later took up tennis. Here he swats the ball during a match with a Japanese minister at a Tokyo hotel in January 1990.**

Yeltsin's own vice president, Aleksandr Rutskoi. Rutskoi, a former army pilot and a hero in the war against Afghanistan, had become disillusioned with Yeltsin's program of economic reform, calling it "economic genocide of the Russian people."[2] Lacking strong leadership qualities himself, Rutskoi was a lightning rod for the anti-Yeltsin forces and to some extent became their tool.

A third contender for power was the radical nationalist and leader of the misnamed Liberal-Democrat party, Vladimir Zhirinovsky. A demagogue who played to the nation's worst impulses—hatred of non-Russians and a hunger for the imperial Russian past— Zhirinovsky had shown he was a power to be reckoned with. He placed third in the June 1991 election for Russian president that Yeltsin had won.

The Russian parliament had an invaluable weapon in its fight against Yeltsin—the Russian constitution. This document, first written in 1918 by the new Soviet government, was revised during Stalin's reign and again in the Brezhnev era. It gave most of the power of government to the parliament, then a mere rubber stamp for the Communist party's Politburo. Yeltsin had a new constitution drafted that called for a presidential republic with a two-house parliament, not unlike the U.S. Congress. The powers of the legislature would be carefully defined and limited, while the president would have far greater executive powers than under the old constitution. The chances of having this new constitution passed by parliament were slim. The legislature would never willingly give up its authority to the president.

As 1992 drew to a close, Russia was in a state of deepening turmoil. Yeltsin and the parliament were deadlocked in their power struggle. Each side ignored the other's decrees and declarations. At times Yeltsin seemed to be holding on to power by his fingernails, hoping against hope that he could keep parliament in check just long enough for the economy to turn the corner and democratic reforms to move forward.

Time seemed to be running out. In late March 1993, the parliament tried to vote Yeltsin out of office. They failed by the slimmest of margins. Yeltsin left for Vancouver, British Columbia, for his first summit meeting with newly elected U.S. President Bill Clinton. Clinton gave Yeltsin his unconditional support in his struggle with the conservatives and pledged millions in aid to Russia if it kept on its democratic course.

Yeltsin returned home to a national vote, or referendum, on his policies. The public expressed its confidence in their president and supported his call for early parliamentary elections. Yeltsin wanted to move the elections up from 1995 to 1993 hoping to break up the majority of Communists and nationalists in parliament. All current members, however, could run for reelection. The proposal was flatly rejected by parliament.

May 1, the traditional Communist May Day, brought more violence as hundreds of Communists turned out in Red Square despite a ban on marching. In confrontations with riot police, one hundred and fifty people were injured.

As the second anniversary of the failed coup arrived, the Russian people were beginning to lose faith in Yeltsin's reforms, which had so far done little to improve their lives. Poverty was more widespread than it had been in decades of Communist rule. Not only were food and consumer goods scarce, but basic med-

━━━━━━━━━━ Yeltsin and newly elected
U.S. President Bill Clinton share an exuberant
moment with a crowd of schoolchildren before
their first summit meeting in Vancouver, Canada,
in April 1993. While Yeltsin was gaining support
from the Americans for his policies, his enemies
at home were plotting his removal from office.

ical supplies and services were inadequate. Aspirin was hard to obtain, let alone more important medicines. Workers' wages were at only 61 percent of what they had been three years earlier. "Before our pensions were small, but it was enough for food, and something extra," said one elderly war veteran. "Now it is just enough for a diet of half-starvation."[3] In a new poll the number of Russians who believed that their lives would be better under capitalism dropped from 29 percent in 1991 to 18 percent. As discontent rose, the dark forces of nationalism and communism grew stronger. Yeltsin was confronted by a difficult decision. Could he use the authority of his office to suspend freedom in order to save his country from chaos? Would he lose the support of the West if he became a temporary dictator to ensure the survival of democracy in Russia?

As summer gave way to fall, Yeltsin made his decision, and the long-awaited showdown between the president and the parliament took place.

CHAPTER TEN

THE UNFOLDING DRAMA

On September 21, 1993, at 8 P.M. President Yeltsin appeared on national television and told the Russian people that "Power in [Parliament] has been seized by a group of persons who have turned it into the head-quarters of irreconcilable opposition."[1] He then an-nounced that he was ordering parliament to be immediately dissolved and calling for the election of a new parliament in December.

Parliament responded in kind. It defied the presi-dent's order to dissolve, voted to depose Yeltsin, and swore in Vice President Rutskoi as acting president. When Yeltsin ignored parliament's actions, their leaders barricaded themselves in the Russian White House. In the next few days, over a thousand parlia-ment supporters camped outside the White House, openly demonstrating against Yeltsin. Parliament's sharp-tongued Speaker, Ruslan Khasbulatov, declared that Yeltsin's "fiendish adventurist policy has brought the country to the verge of civil war."[2]

Not since the failed coup just over two years earlier had Yeltsin faced such a crisis. Only this time, he was on the other side of the barricades. On the second day after Yeltsin's announcement, violence broke out. Armed supporters of parliament attempted to take over the headquarters of the commonwealth military command. A police officer and an innocent bystander were killed.

From inside their barricaded building, Rutskoi and Khasbulatov called for the people to resist Yeltsin and proceeded to set up their own government, complete with cabinet. Yeltsin responded by cutting off the White House's water, electricity, and telephone service. The parliament thought that such actions would win them the sympathy of the Russian people and the Western nations. However, the general public was no more sympathetic to their cause now than they had been before the crisis. They saw parliament as a noisy group of troublemakers out to seize as much power for themselves as possible and passively supported Yeltsin. The Western nations were more emphatic in their support for the Russian president, while getting his pledge not to resort to violence and bloodshed in trying to end the standoff.

Hundreds of soldiers and police, loyal to Yeltsin, surrounded the White House. They called for the parliament members and their supporters inside to surrender their arms and come out peacefully. Yeltsin's only concession to the rebels was to offer to move up the date of his own presidential election from 1996 to 1994.

As the standoff neared the end of its second week, there were no signs of a resolution. When widespread violence finally broke out, it was instigated by the anti-Yeltsin forces. Armed rebels attempted to seize the Moscow television center. Sixty-two people were killed in the fray, many of them innocent bystanders. Yeltsin decided that the time had come to end the siege. He ordered tanks to fire 125-mm shells on the White House. Airborne troops landed atop the building and conducted floor-by-floor assaults. By the late afternoon of October 4, it was over. The defeated parliament members filed out and surrendered. Thirty were arrested, including the two ringleaders, Khasbulatov and Rutskoi. More than 150 people had died in the fighting. It was the worst violence Moscow had seen in years.

Yeltsin had won the bitter struggle with his enemies—at least for the moment. To bring order to the city, he banned some of the opposition political parties and shut down their newspapers. Even *Pravda*, the seventy-year-old Communist journal, was temporarily closed. While curtailing freedom, Yeltsin promised more freedom than Russians had ever known before. The re-drafted constitution, once finished, would extend human rights in nearly every aspect of Russian life. It would also greatly expand the president's powers, while decentralizing the federal government by increasing the power of locally elected legislatures. The new constitution would be voted on in a national referendum to be held on December 12, 1993, the same day as the parliamentary elections. With new executive powers and a more representative parliament, Yeltsin hoped to put his reforms back on track.

The new legislature that Yeltsin proposed would consist of two houses. The lower house, the state Duma, would have 450 deputies. Half of these would be elected directly by the people and half from candidate lists of all parties winning more than 5 percent of the vote. The upper house, the Federal Assembly, would have 176 deputies made up of two candidates elected directly from each of the 88 regions and provinces of Russia.

Political parties were still a novelty in a nation controlled for seventy years by the monolithic Communist party. With only a small percentage of the Russian electorate belonging to a political group, new parties sprang up like mushrooms. But to get its name on the ballot, each party had to get a required 100,000 signatures. Yeltsin himself belonged to no party, but several of his top ministers formed a party called Russia's Choice, that reflected his liberal political views. A more moderate party was formed, called the Russian Party for Unity and Accord, that wanted to slow the pace of reform but not end it. On the left was the Russian Communist party, the only Communist group that had not been banned by Yeltsin. On the right was Zhirinovsky's Liberal Democrat party, which had also managed to survive Yeltsin's ban because Zhirinovsky had supported him against the parliament during the fall crisis.

As the election drew closer, Yeltsin reneged on his promise to move up the presidential election. He said he would stay in office until his full five-year term expired in 1996. Some political rivals saw this as a betrayal of trust to the people, particularly since Yeltsin was limiting the first term of the delegates elected to the new parliament to two years instead of the customary four. Yeltsin believed that he had to complete his full term to assure the continuation of national reform.

Yeltsin took a curiously aloof role in the campaign. He refused to endorse any of the thirteen parties running, even Russia's Choice. He spent all his energies campaigning for the new constitution, which he felt was more important to the future of the country than

━━━━━━━━━━ The greatest threat to Yeltsin's democratic reforms was not a former Communist, but Vladimir Zhirinovsky, an ultra-conservative nationalist. Zhirinovsky's Liberal Democrat Party shocked both Yeltsin's supporters and the world when it won the largest number of votes in the parliamentary election of December 1993.

any political party. "The President, who is elected by the whole population, by all people, by citizens of all regions, is called to personify all Russia, to be the main guarantor of unity," he said in one speech. "But for that he needs corresponding powers."[3] These powers he could only get from a new constitution.

Russia's Choice was expected to win the most votes, but when election day came the result was a stunning upset. Zhirinovsky's Liberal Democrats, who had been derided by most politicians as too extremist to have any wide appeal, won the largest number of votes—nearly 25 percent of all those cast. Russia's Choice came in a sorry second with 14.5 percent. The Russian Communist party was in third place with about 11 percent. It was a shattering blow for Yeltsin's reform policies, but not a total defeat. The new constitution did pass in the referendum, giving Yeltsin the executive powers he needed to keep control of the government.

There were several reasons for Zhirinovsky's strong showing. The votes of many Russians were cast less for Zhirinovsky and his fascist views than they were against Yeltsin's government. People were sick and tired of the high price of reform and were letting Yeltsin know it. The shock tactics of his new economic policies had so far brought little more than misery for the majority of Russians. Over a third of Russia's 150 million people were living in poverty. Inflation was still running high, and while many consumer goods were available on the shelves of Russian shops, few people could afford them. Crime and corruption, once kept in check by an authoritarian Communist state, were running rampant.

Another reason for the upset was Zhirinovsky himself. While other party leaders talked in calm tones of economic growth, Zhirinovsky talked tough on the issues that most concerned many Russians—non-Russians taking over their jobs, the humiliation brought on by the breakup of the Soviet Union, and Russia's diminished status from a superpower to a floundering republic. For all his bombast and outlandish rhetoric, Zhirinovsky came across as an extremely effective candidate on television.

Finally, many liberals blamed Yeltsin himself for Zhirinovsky's triumph. If Yeltsin had endorsed Russia's Choice, they said, and campaigned as vigorously for the party as he had for the constitution, the final vote might have been very different.

Despite the threat of the ultranationalists, they were outnumbered in the new parliament's lower house by Russia's Choice's delegates, 76–63. But the Liberal Democrats with the Communists and their conservative allies held nearly 40 percent of the Duma's 450 votes. They could effectively block reform legislation and turn the state Duma into the same troublesome body the old parliament was, although without its former power.

What would come next for Russia? Would Yeltsin preside over the rebirth of a democratic Russian state, or would the old autocratic Russia of the czars and the Communists return? Would Russia, exhausted by reform, turn its back on democracy and embrace a new imperialism, much as Germany, under the spell of Adolf Hitler, did in the 1930s after the failure of democracy there? Would Zhirinovsky's call to rebuild the Russian Empire and take Alaska back from the Americans prove to be hot air or a blueprint for the future?

Yeltsin claimed that Russia would not become another Nazi Germany, that he and the constitution stood between Russia and the antidemocratic forces in his

━━━━━━━━━━ One of Boris Yeltsin's greatest
strengths has been his ability to identify with
common people. Here he talks with a group
of citizens on a crowded Moscow street in
April 1993. Have the people's complaints
about the economic and social problems
caused by his reforms led him to slow the
changeover to a market economy?

[93]

country. But the constitution alone would not be enough to stay the course. Without vital democratic institutions, such as a strong judiciary and a balanced legislature, the roots of a Russian democracy could wither before they took hold.

A strong presidency may be important to establishing democracy as long as a man like Yeltsin is in office. But such overriding power in the wrong hands could put Russia under a dictatorship as terrible as Stalin's. It is disturbing to hear that Zhirinovsky strongly supports Yeltsin's new constitution, knowing full well the power it would give him if he were to be elected the next president.

Recent events show Yeltsin to be more willing to compromise his position in the face of political reality. Yeltsin's moderate prime minister Viktor Chernomyrdin, with Yeltsin's consent, put the brakes on reform, claiming that "the mechanical transfer of Western economic methods to Russian soil has done more harm than good."[4] In response to this shift to the right, Yegor Gaidar, the chief architect of Yeltsin's economic policy, and Finance Minister Boris Fyodorov, both resigned from the government. Yeltsin immediately appointed several more moderate, if not conservative, men to his cabinet.

Would Yeltsin make the same mistake Gorbachev did by putting the brakes on progress to save his government from attack by his political enemies? Or would this serve as a deliberate political move to form a united bloc of liberals and moderates to hold the nationalists and Communists in check?

In his first summit meeting with President Bill Clinton in January 1994, Yeltsin assured the U.S. leader: "We are not going to reverse our reform course. But we do want to cushion the impact of it."[5] Gaidar and

President Yeltsin and President Clinton shake hands in the White House on September 28, 1994. During his welcoming speech, Clinton said of this summit meeting of the super powers: "Today, we meet not as adversaries but as partners in the quest for a more prosperous and peaceful planet."[6]

Fyodorov, however, believed that slowing the reforms would rob them of all impact and prolong the misery rather than alleviate it. In moving too slowly, Yeltsin might also run the risk of losing his mandate for change.

The road that Yeltsin and Russia were traveling was a dangerous one. The United States and other Western countries could offer support and aid, but in the final analysis it would be up to the Russian people to decide their own fate. It would not be an easy decision.

And what ultimate role would Boris Yeltsin, the maverick who turned from communism to democracy, play in this unfolding drama?

"Those who expect him to act like an American or Western European politician rather than as a product of Russian political culture will remain skeptical," writes John Morrison. "But whether he can meet the broader challenge of governing democratically, of making democracy work in Russia, is more of an open question. If Yeltsin, with such great popular support, fails, then the chances of anyone else succeeding are slim."[7]

Time and again, Boris Yeltsin has gone up against impossible odds. Through courage, fortitude, and sheer stubbornness, he has triumphed. He is now facing what is surely the biggest challenge of his career. Whether he succeeds or fails, he will put up a good fight. It is the fight, the struggle, that he lives for. The good news is that, like his beloved Russia, Boris Yeltsin is not only a fighter but a survivor.

CHRONOLOGY

1931   Boris Nikolayevich Yeltsin is born in Butko, a village in Sverdlovsk province of the Soviet Union (Feb. 1).

1949   Enters the Urals Polytechnic Institute.

1955   After college graduation is assigned a job as a construction boss in Sverdlovsk.

1956   Marries Naina (Naya) Girin.

1957   His first daughter, Lena, is born.

1959   His second daughter, Tanya, is born.

1961   Joins the Communist party.

1963   Becomes manager of prefabricated housing construction company for city of Sverdlovsk.

1969   Appointed head of construction section of the Sverdlovsk provincial party committee.

1976   Becomes first secretary of the provincial committee.

1982   Soviet leader Leonid Brezhnev dies, and Yuri Andropov becomes new leader (November).

1984   Andropov dies and is succeeded by Konstantin Chernenko (February).

1985   Mikhail Gorbachev becomes the new Soviet leader (March).

Yeltsin comes to Moscow as head of the Central Committee's construction department (July).

Becomes Moscow first party secretary (December).

1987   Speaks out against slow pace of Gorbachev's reforms at Central Committee meeting and is attacked by Gorbachev and others (Oct. 21).

"Confesses" his errors before Gorbachev at a Moscow party committee meeting and is later demoted back to the construction section (November).

1988   Pleads for his rehabilitation at 19th Conference and wins the support of the public (July 1).

1989   Wins election to People's Congress of Deputies in the first democratic election in the Soviet Union in 70 years (March).

Elected to Supreme Soviet, permanent governing body made up of deputies from the Congress of Deputies (May).

Makes first visit to the United States (September).

1990   Elected chairman of the Russian Supreme Council (July).

Resigns from Communist party at the 28th Party Congress in Moscow (July 12).

1991	Gorbachev declares a state of emergency in Lithuania after Soviet troops fire on demonstrators (Feb. 1).

Yeltsin is elected president of Russia (June 12).

Three-day coup of conservatives in Gorbachev's government ends in failure (August 19–21).

Russia and two other republics sign Minsk Agreement, decreeing that the Soviet Union has ceased to exist (Dec. 8).

Eleven of the fifteen republics of the former Soviet Union form the Commonwealth of Independent States (CIS) (Dec. 21).

1992 The Soviet Union dissolves, and Gorbachev resigns as its president (Jan. 1).

Yeltsin has his first summit meeting with U.S. President George Bush (June).

1993 The Russian parliament tries to vote Yeltsin out of office, but fails (March).

Yeltsin orders the dissolution of parliament and calls for new elections in December (Sept. 21).

Parliament members barricade themselves in the Russian White House until Yeltsin's troops force them out. About 150 people are killed (Sept. 22–Oct. 4).

Vladimir Zhirinovsky's Liberal Democrat party wins the most votes in a stunning upset in parliamentary elections (December).

1994 Yeltsin accepts the resignations of two of his top aides and appoints more conservative politicians to his cabinet (January).

Yeltsin joins U.S. President Bill Clinton for a summit meeting at the White House (Sept. 27–28).

NOTES

Chapter One

1. *Time*, Sept. 2, 1991.
2. John Morrison, *Boris Yeltsin: From Bolshevik to Democrat* (New York: Dutton, 1991), pp. 283–284.
3. Ibid., p. 286.

Chapter Two

1. Boris Yeltsin, *Against the Grain* (New York: Summit Books, 1990), p. 22.
2. Ibid., p. 24.
3. Vladimir Solovyov and Elena Klepikova, *Boris Yeltsin: A Political Biography* (New York: Putnam, 1992), p. 20.
4. *Current Biography Yearbook 1989* (New York: H. W. Wilson Co., 1989), p. 645.
5. Yeltsin, p. 29.
6. Ibid., p. 29.
7. Ibid., p. 36.
8. Ibid., p. 37.
9. Ibid., p. 37.
10. Ibid., p. 93

Chapter Three

1. Yeltsin, p. 44.
2. Ibid., p. 45.

3. Solovyov and Klepikova, p. 134.
4. Yeltsin, p. 51.
5. Morrison, p. 36.
6. Yeltsin, p. 64.

Chapter Four

1. Yeltsin, p. 80.
2. Solovyov and Klepikova, p. 146.
3. Yeltsin, p. 67.
4. Ibid., pp. 69–70.
5. Ibid., p. 72.

Chapter Five

1. Yeltsin, p. 108.
2. Solovyov and Klepikova, p. 31.
3. *Current Biography Yearbook 1989*, p. 645.
4. Solovyov and Klepikova, p. 51.
5. Yeltsin, p. 121.
6. Ibid., pp. 182–183.
7. Solovyov and Klepikova, p. 57.
8. Ibid., p. 50.

Chapter Six

1. Yeltsin, p. 192.
2. Morrison, p. 63.
3. Ibid., p. 64.
4. Solovyov and Klepikova, p. 65.
5. Morrison, p. 64.
6. Yeltsin, p. 187.
7. Morrison, p. 67.
8. Ibid., pp. 67–68.
9. Solovyov and Klepikova, p. 67.
10. Ibid., p. 68.
11. Morrison, p. 71.
12. *Current Biography Yearbook 1989*, p. 646.
13. Ibid., p. 647.

14. Yeltsin, pp. 204–205.
15. Ibid., p. 204.
16. Solovyov and Klepikova, p. 78.

Chapter Seven

1. Yeltsin, p. 14.
2. Solovyov and Klepikova, p. 92.
3. Ibid., p. 97.
4. Ibid., p. 99.
5. Ibid., p. 161.
7. Ibid., p. 171.
8. Yeltsin, p. 255.
9. Solovyov and Klepikova, p. 173.
10. Ibid., p. 175.

Chapter Eight

1. Solovyov and Klepikova, pp. 195–196.
2. Ibid., p. 208.
3. Ibid., pp. 225–226.
4. *Newsweek*, June 24, 1991.
5. Solovyov and Klepikova, p. 220.

Chapter Nine

1. Wright, John W., editor, *The Universal Almanac 1993* (Kansas City, Missouri: Universal Press, 1992), p. 492.
2. *Time*, March 9, 1992.
3. *The New York Times*, November 12, 1993.

Chapter Ten

1. *The New York Times*, September 22, 1993.
2. *The Connecticut Post*, September 24, 1993.
3. *The New York Times*, December 9, 1993.
4. Ibid., January 22, 1994.
5. Ibid., January 17, 1994.
6. *The New York Times*, September 27, 1994.
7. Morrison, p. 290.

BIBLIOGRAPHY

Gwertzman, Bernard, and Kaufman, Michael T. *The Collapse of Communism*. New York: Random House, 1990. (An engrossing narrative of the fervent days of communism's fall in the Soviet Union and Eastern Europe as seen through the eyes of *The New York Times* journalists stationed in each country.)

Morrison, John. *Boris Yeltsin: From Bolshevik to Democrat*. New York: Dutton, 1991. (A well-researched biography that concentrates on Yeltsin's career since the mid-1980s and gives an abbreviated version of his earlier life.)

Solovyov, Vladimir, and Klepikova, Elena. *Boris Yeltsin: A Political Biography*. New York: Putnam, 1992. (This biography by two Russian insiders parallels Yeltsin's career with that of Gorbachev. Their tendency to blame all Russia's ills on Gorbachev mar an otherwise excellent book.)

Yeltsin, Boris. *Against the Grain*. New York: Summit Books, 1990. (This "official" autobiography is something of a disappointment. Yeltsin's humdrum writing captures little of the charisma of the man and gives few insights into his life. Still, it is worthwhile reading for anyone who is interested in the Russian leader.)

INDEX

Esalen Institute, 65
Estonia, 69, 78

Federal Assembly, 88
Free market economy, 42, 76, 79
Fyodorov, Boris, 94

Gaidar, Yegor, 94
Georgia, 78, 79
Glasnost, 42, 46
Gorbachev, Mikhail, *57*
   coup d'état (1991) and, 9–10, 13, 14, 76
   foreign policy and, 65
   reforms of, 42, 44, 46, 48, 69, 71
   republics question, 69–70, 72
   resignation of, 78
   succeeds Chernenko, 40
   Yeltsin and, 38–40, 42, 44, 48–50, 52–56, 59, 61, 63, 72, 78
Gosstroi, 56, 59
Grishin, Viktor, 44

Harrison, James, 65, 66
Hitler, Adolf, 92
Housing, 25, 27, 33
Hungary, 69

Jaruzelski, Wojciech, 55

Kapital, Das (Marx), 27, 28
Karelian Autonomous
   Republic, 61

Kazannik, Yuri, 63
KGB, 38
Khasbulatov, Ruslan, 81, 86–88
Khrushchev, Nikita, 25, *26*, 30, 60
Klepikova, Elena, 59
Kolkhoz, 16
Komsomol, 38
Kravchenko, Leonid, 9
Kyrgyzstan, 77

Landsbergis, Vytautas, 71
Latvia, 69, 78
Leningrad, 44, 58
Liberal Democrat party, 82, 89, 91–92
Ligachev, Yegor, 41, 51–53, 61
Limitchiki, 47
Lithuania, 69–72, 78

Major, John, 11
Manuakin, Sergei, 53
Marx, Karl, 27, 28
Meat market, *37*
Minsk Agreement (1991), 78
Moldova, 77
Morrison, John, 34, 96
Moscow, 44, *45*, 47–48
Moscow State University, 58

19th Party Conference (1988), 60–61

October Revolution, 51

Pamyat, 49